# ZPL

# Moose

## By JoAnn Early Macken

**Reading Consultant:** Jeanne Clidas, Ph.D.
Director, Roberts Wesleyan College Literacy Clinic

**WEEKLY READER®**
PUBLISHING

Please visit our web site at **www.garethstevens.com**.
For a free catalog describing our list of high-quality books,
call 1-877-542-2595 (USA) or 1-800-387-3178 (Canada).
Our fax: 1-877-542-2596

**Library of Congress Cataloging-in-Publication Data**

Macken, JoAnn Early, 1953–
    Moose / by JoAnn Early Macken.
       p. cm. — (Animals that live in the forest)
    Includes bibliographical references and index.
    ISBN-10: 1-4339-2404-8   ISBN-13: 978-1-4339-2404-0 (lib. bdg.)
    ISBN-10: 1-4339-2480-3   ISBN-13: 978-1-4339-2480-4 (soft cover)
    1. Moose—Juvenile literature. I. Title.
  QL737.U55M256   2010
  599.65'7–dc22                   2009001929

This edition first published in 2010 by
**Weekly Reader® Books**
An Imprint of Gareth Stevens Publishing
1 Reader's Digest Road
Pleasantville, NY  10570-7000 USA

Copyright © 2010 by Gareth Stevens, Inc.

Executive Managing Editor: Lisa M. Herrington
Senior Editor: Barbara Bakowski
Project Management: Spooky Cheetah Press
Cover Designers: Jennifer Ryder-Talbot and Studio Montage
Production: Studio Montage
Library Consultant: Carl Harvey, Library Media Specialist, Noblesville, Indiana

Photo credits: Cover, p. 1: Shutterstock; pp. 5, 19 © Alan and Sandy Carey; pp. 7, 9, 11, 13, 15, 17, 21
© Michael H. Francis

Printed in the United States of America

1 2 3 4 5 6 7 8 9 14 13 12 11 10 09

# Table of Contents

**Boldface** words appear in the glossary.

## Mothers and Babies

A moose **calf** hides in the forest. The baby's light brown fur blends in with the trees. Older moose may have darker fur.

calf

For its first few weeks, a calf drinks its mother's milk. A grown female moose is called a **cow**.

A calf can walk soon after it is born. In a short time, it can run and swim. It eats plants. Its mother stays close to watch for danger.

Moose have good hearing. A moose can turn one ear at a time. Moose also have a good sense of smell. These sharp senses help keep moose safe.

ears

## Changing With the Seasons

Male moose grow **antlers** each spring. The antlers fall off in winter. As the moose grows older, the antlers grow bigger.

antlers

In summer, moose stay near water. They swim to get away from danger. They eat water lilies and other plants. They dive down to find food.

In winter, moose eat tree bark and needles. Their long legs help them walk through deep snow. Their fur keeps them warm.

## Food for Later

Moose spend most of their time eating. They swallow their food right away. They bring up the food to chew it later! The food they chew later is called their **cud**.

Moose live alone for most of the year. In winter, they may look for food in groups.

# Fast Facts

| | |
|---|---|
| **Height** | about 7 feet (2 meters) at the shoulder |
| **Length** | about 10 feet (3 meters) nose to tail |
| **Weight** | Males: about 1,600 pounds (726 kilograms)<br>Females: about 1,300 pounds (590 kilograms) |
| **Diet** | leaves, twigs, grass, and water plants |
| **Average life span** | up to 15 years |

# Glossary

**antlers:** the branched horns of animals in the deer family

**calf:** a baby moose or other animal such as a cow, an elephant, and a whale

**cow:** a grown female moose

**cud:** food that has been swallowed and brought up to be chewed again

# For More Information

## Books

*It's a Baby Moose!* Baby Mammals (series). Kelly Doudna (SandCastle, 2008)

*Moose.* A True Book (series). Ann O. Squire (Children's Press, 2007)

## Web Sites

### Moose
*animals.nationalgeographic.com/animals/mammals/moose.html*
Hear a real moose call, and print out your own fact sheet.

### Mooseworld for Kids
*www.mooseworld.com/forkids.htm*
Find fun games, crafts, and puzzles.

# Index

## About the Author

JoAnn Early Macken is the author of two rhyming picture books, *Sing-Along Song* and *Cats on Judy,* and more than 80 nonfiction books for children. Her poems have appeared in several children's magazines. She lives in Wisconsin with her husband and their two sons.